Every Last Drop

BRINGING CLEAN WATER HOME

MICHELLE MULDER

ORCA BOOK PUBLISHERS

Library and Archives Canada Cataloguing in Publication

Mulder, Michelle, 1976-, author
Every last drop : bringing clean water home / Michelle Mulder.
(Orca footprints)

Includes bibliographical references and index.
Issued also in electronic format.

ISBN 978-1-4598-0223-0 (bound).--ISBN 978-1-4598-0224-7 (pdf).--
ISBN 978-1-4598-0712-9 (epub)

1. Water quality management--Juvenile literature. 2. Water
resources development--Juvenile literature. I. Title.
II. Series: Orca footprints

HD1691.M84 2014   j333.91   c2013-906646-2
c2013-906647-0

First published in the United States, 2014
Library of Congress Control Number: 2013951377

Summary: Clean water is a precious resource in a thirsty world.

Orca Book Publishers is dedicated to preserving the environment and has printed this book on Forest Stewardship Council® certified paper.

Orca Book Publishers gratefully acknowledges the support for its publishing programs provided by the following agencies: the Government of Canada through the Canada Book Fund and the Canada Council for the Arts, and the Province of British Columbia through the BC Arts Council and the Book Publishing Tax Credit.

Cover images by Getty Images and Dreamstime
Back cover images (top left to right): Gastón Castaño, Jim Holmes, Green Empowerment/Evan Sabogal; (bottom left to right): Centre for Affordable Water & Sanitation Technology (CAWST), Dreamstime, Getty Images

Design and production by Teresa Bubela and Jenn Playford

ORCA BOOK PUBLISHERS
PO Box 5626, STN. B
Victoria, BC Canada
V8R 6S4

ORCA BOOK PUBLISHERS
PO Box 468
Custer, WA USA
98240-0468

www.orcabook.com
Printed and bound in Canada.

17 16 15 14 • 4 3 2 1

Ninety-seven percent of Earth's water is in our oceans. Fresh water—like this spring in São Tomé and Principe—is precious.
GETTY IMAGES

For Mel

Contents

CHAPTER ONE:
A DROP TO DRINK

CHAPTER TWO:
RIDING THE WATER CYCLE

CHAPTER THREE:
PUMP IT UP

CHAPTER FOUR:
DEEPENING THE WELL

Introduction

Have you ever been to a place where it's dangerous to rinse your toothbrush under the tap?

When I was twenty-three, I visited my friend Mel, who had volunteered to lead development groups in Peru. For two months I hiked with her to tiny settlements in the mountains, worked on my Spanish, and even tried making bread in an adobe oven.

Then, suddenly, I got very sick. For days I spent almost all my time in the bathroom. Mel borrowed a truck to drive me three hours to the nearest hospital, and medical tests showed that bacteria (germs) from our water had multiplied in my digestive system. Antibiotics—and an intravenous drip that rehydrated my body—saved my life.

Not everyone is so lucky. Every day thousands of people—most of them children—die because they've drunk dirty water (or they don't have clean water to wash with) and they can't get to a doctor. The good news is that it doesn't have to be this way. Around the world, people are finding creative ways to collect and clean all the water they need. Did you know that some families in Botswana use solar power to turn salt water into fresh water? Or that some folks in Chile use huge nets to catch fog that becomes clean drinking water? And at schools in several places, kids collect clean water by playing on playground-powered water pumps!

Everyone on the planet has a right to clean water, and people are working hard to make this a reality. Want to find out more? Grab a water bottle, and come with me!

Me, Mel and Padre David, the priest who hosted us in Pamparomas, Peru. Mel and I were about to begin a hike up the mountains to visit the lake that provides the town with its water. MELANIE FRICOT

These lakes, high in the mountains above Pamparomas, are the local drinking water source. The lakes were first built hundreds of years ago, then fell into disrepair and were recently reconstructed. MICHELLE MULDER

Go with the Flow

When I got sick in Peru, the news spread through the town quickly, and soon people appeared at our door with traditional remedies. Meanwhile, Mel whipped up more salty banana milkshakes than I'd ever imagined. (Yes, they were just as disgusting as they sound, but we knew that I needed to drink sugar, salt and fluids to get better.) In the end, it was Mel's access to a truck and hospital that saved my life. Happily, I've never had to drink a salty milkshake since.

In this tiny settlement in rural Peru, people get their drinking water from a stream that runs between the houses. You can see it here at the bottom of the photo. MICHELLE MULDER

CHAPTER ONE

A Drop to Drink

SLURP IT UP, BUTTERCUP

If your family decided to move, what would you look for in a new place? A big living room? A school, playground, library or shops nearby? Thousands of years ago—and even today, in many places—the first thing you'd look for was the nearest lake or river.

Every living thing needs water to survive. (And if you've ever swallowed salt water when swimming in the ocean, you know that not just any water will do. We need fresh, clean water.) Early humans slurped from rivers and lakes, using their hands as cups. These days, many people can drink a glass of water right in their own homes, simply by turning on a tap. How did we get here from there? The story begins about 12,000 years ago, with the planting of a seed.

When you don't have a water tap nearby, rivers and lakes are crucial. These families in Morocco wash clothes in their local river.
HENRY MULDER

HEY, WATER! COME THIS WAY!

Imagine waking up to the birds twittering and your stomach rumbling. You crawl out of bed to look for something to eat—not in the fridge, but in the bush outside your tent. A little while later, you're chewing on a chunk of meat and tossing back a few berries.

This underground cistern in Istanbul, Turkey, was built 1,400 years ago by over 7,000 slaves. GIOVANNI DE CARO/DREAMSTIME.COM

For hundreds of thousands of years, people followed their food everywhere. If those antelopes (that your mom turned into amazing steaks) ran across the grassy plains in summertime, your family was there to meet (and eat) them. If those delicious purple berries grew in the river valley every September, you got there in time to pick as many as you could.

About 12,000 years ago, people in the Near East (western Asia) began to help nature along a bit. When they found a plant they liked, they cleared space to let it grow and brought the plant more water from the nearest lake or river. The plants grew bigger and yielded more food.

Soon, people stopped following their food around and stayed in one place, planting and tending their crops. Lugging water got exhausting, so they invented other ways to bring water to their plants. Some built big basins, called *cisterns*, to collect rainwater.

WATER FACT: A person can live for weeks without food, but only a few days without water. The human brain is 75 percent water. Blood has even more water in it, and even our bones are 20 percent water. No wonder we need to drink so often!

Using wells for drinking water isn't just a thing of the past. Many families around the world, like this one in Guinea Bissau in western Africa, rely on them for all their water needs.
POTTERS WITHOUT BORDERS

Some tried to divert rivers or streams by digging channels to their crops. Others dug tunnels from rivers to fields. In fact, if you were a farmer's kid thousands of years ago, digging tunnels might have been your chore, since kids are small enough to get through tunnels easily. Sudden gushes of water and collapsing tunnels made this a risky job, though.

WELL, WELL, WELL

Much of Earth is covered in water, but did you know that a lot of water is underground too?

About 9,000 years ago, people began to dig wells—deep pits, usually lined with bricks, stones, or even wickerwork. The earliest well that we know about is in what is now the Mediterranean island of Cyprus. The wells were great for drinking water, but not so great for watering crops. Imagine watering an entire field with a bucket. People who relied on wells for irrigation didn't have very big fields.

WATER FACT: Canada has less than 1 percent of Earth's population but enjoys 20 percent of its available fresh water. China has 20 percent of the world's population and only 7 percent of its fresh water.

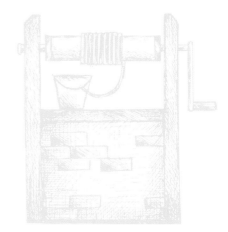

Go with the Flow

When my friend Mel and I visited Chunya, high up in the mountains of Peru, we paid special attention to where we walked. The ditches bringing drinking water from the mountains run right through the settlement, and goats roam free between houses. They particularly enjoy resting near the communal latrines or outhouses it seems, which made going to the latrine in the black of night an adventure-filled experience. Mind the goat!

A Peruvian woman cooks with water that she scoops up from the water channel in the ground beside her. MELANIE FRICOT

For the ancient Greeks, fig trees were like giant billboards announcing underground water. Fig and rosemary plants only grow where water runs underground, so spotting them was cause for celebration.
NICHOLAS RJABOW/DREAMSTIME.COM

The aqueduct in the distance looks like a bridge, but it carried water instead of people or cars. VIATOR

But people who diverted rivers and lakes did. By 6,500 years ago, people in Egypt and southern Mesopotamia (now Iraq and parts of Syria, Turkey and Iran) had large fields that grew plenty of food. With more food available, more and more people could live in the same place, and as a result, cities were built and civilizations began.

THE FORGOTTEN FLUSH

If you lived in the Minoan palace of Knossos on the island of Crete 3,600 years ago, you would have enjoyed fountains, gardens, running water, and even a flush toilet—luxuries that only became common in North America and Europe a hundred years ago.

How did the Minoans do it? They built *aqueducts*—bridges for carrying water—from a spring about 0.5 kilometers (one-third of a mile) away. Baked-clay pipes beneath the palace carried water in and out of the building. But then an earthquake demolished the palace, and another civilization called the Mycenaeans conquered the Minoans. If only the conquerors had asked for plumbing lessons before they destroyed Minoan civilization, the future of humanity might have been very different. But more about that later in this chapter.

SCRUB-A-DUB

After the Mycenaeans conquered the Minoans, people in and around Greece forgot about plumbing for about a thousand years, and then the ancient Greeks started building aqueducts. They also had strict rules about conserving water and reusing washing water for things like watering crops.

When the Romans conquered the Greeks, about 2,300 years ago, they took one look at Greek aqueducts and decided to build even bigger ones everywhere they went. Some of those aqueducts were 100 kilometers (62 miles) long and were powered only by gravity. The result? Water that flowed constantly in all of Rome's major cities.

Why did Romans need constantly running water? The answer might surprise you: Romans loved nothing more than a long hot bath…in public! Men or women gathered in bathhouses to wash themselves, chat and enjoy entertainment, and water from the baths was reused to flush out sewage from the public toilets that were usually next door. The Roman custom of public bathing lasted for hundreds of years, and public baths are still common in some countries, like Turkey.

THREE CHEERS FOR GRAVITY!

While the Greeks and Romans were reinventing aqueducts, how were people getting water in the rest of the world?

Well, in the area that is now Iran, after years of digging down to find water underground, people decided to try something new: digging sideways. The first *qanat* (pronounced ke-**nat**)—as the tunnels into the sides of hills were called—was documented 2,700 years ago, and the idea was so popular that visitors to the area brought the idea to North Africa and Spain. The Spanish brought qanats to Mexico, where people built them for a long time too.

Designing a qanat was no easy job, though. If you were the son of a qanat designer, learning from your father, you would first have to find an underground lake or pond called an *aquifer*. Then you would dig a long tunnel and a series of shafts from

At public toilets in ancient Rome, twenty to forty people sat together to do their business. And the experience wasn't the only thing they shared. Since no one had invented toilet paper yet, people cleaned their backsides with toilet sponges, which they rinsed out in running water and left for the next person to use!
ASTRID228/DREAMSTIME.COM

WATER FACT: Rome's first sewer, called Cloaca Maxima, was built about 2,600 years ago and still flows under the city's streets.

Over 4,000 years ago, people discovered that boiling their drinking water kept them from getting sick. Then they discovered that pouring boiling water over plant leaves made the water taste better. That's how tea was invented, and it's now an important part of many cultures around the world.
MICHELLE MULDER

the aquifer to a farmer's field. (And we're not talking a few meters of tunnel, either. Some qanats are thirty-two kilometers, or twenty miles, long!) If you angled everything perfectly, gravity would channel the water to the field at just the right speed. The farmer would be thrilled. And if you didn't get killed by a collapsing or flooded tunnel while you built your qanat, you and your dad would be very relieved.

In Iran, many farmers still use qanats because they run on gravity, the cheapest power source around. All over the world, and throughout history, people have invented brilliant ways to direct water to where they needed it. In China over 2,000 years ago, people used woven bamboo baskets and stones to redirect a river. Around the same time, in what is now Peru, the Nasca people developed qanat-like irrigation called *puquios* (pronounced poo-**key**-ose), and people use puquios to this day.

Go with the Flow

When I was nineteen, I spent a summer in a remote village in the Dominican Republic. I was part of a team of Canadian volunteers helping to dig a trench for a water pipeline. Before we arrived, the villagers scrubbed down the two-room school and set up metal bunk beds for us there. They also built this shower out back. None of the villagers had such a fancy setup (most bathed at a water tap or in the river, I imagine), but the thirteen of us who shared this shower were grateful for it after a long hot day of digging.

This simple shower is a one-of-a-kind luxury in a tiny village in the Dominican Republic.
MICHELLE MULDER

One thousand years ago, the Mayans of Central America dug huge water reservoirs (human-made lakes to collect water), some of them 100 meters (109 yards) wide. This book would have to be as big as a boat to cover all the clever ways that people have managed water through time.

LOOK OUT BELOW

Unfortunately, not all cultures have been so creative in getting rid of water—wastewater, that is. For example, after the fall of the Roman Empire about 1,500 years ago, most people in Europe gave up on the Roman sewer system and bathhouses. Why? One theory says the Christian church was disgusted by the idea of men and women hanging out naked together in public. So Christians stopped bathing. In fact, some historians say that, since the Muslims and Jews continued bathing regularly, being dirty became a sign of being a good Christian!

Without water from public baths to flush out toilets, people also changed their toilet habits. Many people pooped a little way from where they lived and just left it there to stink. Others did their business in a bowl called a chamber pot and then tossed the contents out the window. Imagine doing that as your friends and neighbors wandered around below!

FULL STEAM AHEAD!

Water's a funny thing. You need to drink it to live, but if it enters your lungs, you can drown. Every time people dug shafts and tunnels into the ground to find water, diggers risked drowning in a flood.

In the Middle Ages in Europe, diggers ran this risk not to find water, but to find coal. Several hundred years ago, people in Europe were running out of trees for firewood and began using

"Garderobe" is a fancy name for the bathroom of a medieval castle. Human waste fell right into the moat below. So don't believe stories you've heard about moats filled with crocodiles. Those floating brown lumps weren't animals after all!
DAVE DUNFORD/WIKIPEDIA

Walking along the sidewalk in England could be a messy business 500 years ago. You never knew when someone might empty a chamber pot on your head!
BRIDGEMAN ART LIBRARY

15

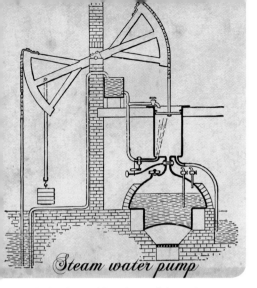

Steam water pump

This simple machine changed the entire course of history!
DARKO VESELINOVIC/DREAMSTIME.COM

coal instead. Miners dug black lumps of the fossil fuel from deep underground. Sometimes they hit water, and their pits and tunnels flooded, killing everyone inside.

In 1769, James Watt developed the first functional steam engine to pump water out of flooded coal mines. His pump changed the world forever. Businessmen began building factories all over England, using steam engines to power their machines. This was the Industrial Revolution. Huge numbers of people moved from the countryside to work in new factories. Cities got bigger and needed more and more fresh water.

THE GREAT STINK

More people meant more waste, and it wasn't just poop. Leather workers, cloth makers, potters, butchers and others would toss waste from their small businesses out the window or into the nearest stream.

In 1858 in London, the waste of three million people flowed into the Thames River and brought it to a standstill. That summer was extra warm, and the stink of the water was so terrible that the House of Commons hung bleach-soaked cloths in the windows so the lawmakers could breathe. It didn't help much, so within eighteen days the members of parliament officially decided to build a massive sewer system…kind of like the one built under Rome over 2,000 years earlier.

GUSHING AWAY

Three times more people live on our planet today than 100 years ago. But we're using six times as much water. Why? Well, for one thing, since Mr. Watt invented his steam engine, people have invented other machines that pump water even more efficiently.

DIRTY FATHER THAMES.

Ten years before the Great Stink, cartoonists were already pointing out how dirty London's Thames River was.
BRIDGEMAN ART LIBRARY

Sometimes, when something is easier to get, it seems less precious and we don't look after it as much.

For instance, both mining and farming now use more water than ever before, and both industries can release toxins or poisons into local water supplies. On top of that, almost every product we buy has passed through a factory at some point, and factories use plenty of water too.

For centuries, people have been using water as if we have a limitless supply. Meanwhile, climate change is affecting how much rain each part of the world gets, and every year more and more people run out of clean water to drink. How is this possible? And more importantly, what are we doing to solve the problem?

A hundred years ago, schools in North America rarely had running water. Each day a different student brought enough water for all the students in the school to share. GLENBOW ARCHIVES, NA-863-3

Without a water tap at home, your laundry day might look like this one in Alberta, Canada, a hundred years ago. First, haul water home in barrels. Then heat it on the stove. And then scrub all your clothing by hand. GLENBOW ARCHIVES, NA-1872-1

CHAPTER TWO

Riding the Water Cycle

WATER, WATER, EVERYWHERE

Ever wonder why we call our planet "Earth" when most of it is covered in water? It's kind of funny when you think about it.

Not to brag, but we've got more water than any other planet in our solar system, and water means life. All living things need water. It dissolves minerals and nutrients from our food and carries them around our bodies. When you water a plant, the water dissolves minerals in the soil. The plant's roots draw up that mineral-rich water. Then the leaves blend the water, minerals and air with energy from the sun to make nutrients. These nutrients feed the plant. When you eat plants, your blood (which is mostly water) transports the plants' nutrients throughout your body.

But our watery planet with the funny name doesn't have a limitless supply of drinking water. In fact, 97 percent of Earth's water is in our oceans—*blech!* Salt water! Totally undrinkable!—and most of what's left is trapped in glaciers and ice caps. Of all the water on the planet, only 1 percent is fresh water that plants and animals, like us, can drink. If it weren't for the fresh water of rivers, lakes and streams, we wouldn't have a drop to drink!

Funny how we call such a watery planet Earth! CORNELIUS20/DREAMSTIME.COM

Around the world, most glaciers are melting at an astounding rate. GASTÓN CASTAÑO

DINOSAUR DRINKS

Did you know that you've probably drunk some of the same water that a dinosaur sipped from a puddle a few million years ago? We've had the same amount of water on the planet for two billion years. It's constantly recycled in a big natural system called the *water cycle*.

How does the water cycle work? The sun heats Earth's water, and when water gets hot, it turns to vapor. Up it floats into the air, and then—*bam!*—it hits colder air and condenses into clouds. When the clouds get heavy with all that water, the water falls back to Earth, either as rain or snow. Some of that rain goes right back into oceans, lakes and streams. Some sinks into the soil, and some seeps so far down into the ground

WATER FACT: Imagine all the water of the world in a four-liter (one-gallon) bucket. Only a tablespoonful would be drinkable fresh water.

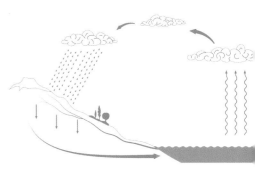

Monsoon season in Thailand has always meant a lot of rain. In 2011, monsoons caused dangerous flooding. THOR JORGEN UDVANG/DREAMSTIME.COM

In 1978, Iguazú Falls in Argentina dried up for 28 days. Imagine all this water evaporating, leaving only dry soil. GASTÓN CASTAÑO

that it collects as an aquifer or underground lake. (Aquifers take thousands of years to form, and aquifer water can remain underground for hundreds of years.) Some of the water that falls as snow becomes part of the world's glaciers or polar ice. The cycle repeats constantly and has done so for billions of years.

But recently, with global warming, climates around the world have begun to change. The polar ice is melting and flowing into the ocean. Some parts of the planet are receiving more rain than ever before; people are flooded out of their homes, and water reservoirs might be filled with dirty runoff. In other places, rain hardly falls at all anymore, and lakes, streams and even rivers are drying up. Water sources that people have relied on for thousands of years are changing.

SWAMPING THE SWAMPS

Turn on a tap. Fill up a glass with water. Admire this liquid that's been around for billions of years. Animals have bathed in it. It's been through the mud. Maybe it's even sloshed around a toilet bowl at some point. And we *drink* that stuff!?

Before you vow never to drink another drop again, remember that people existed in the world for thousands of years before anyone invented water filters. That's because nature has its own filtration system. It's called a wetland.

A wetland is a marsh or swamp or any area of land where the soil near the surface is covered with water. The soil in these places acts like a pollution filter. Contaminants that pollute the water attach to sand or organic material. Bacteria break down nutrients and feed them back into the ecosystem.

Wetlands like this one inspired the first water treatment plants.
BRONWYN8/DREAMSTIME.COM

Go with the Flow

I saw shrines like this one all over Argentina when I traveled there with my husband. Legend has it that over 150 years ago, a woman crossing the desert with her baby died of thirst on the way. But her baby survived "miraculously" by nursing for days after the mother had died. The woman has become a local saint, and people throughout Argentina, Chile and Uruguay ask la Difunta Correa to help them reach their goals. In thanks, they leave a bottle of water at one of the roadside shrines.

These bottles of water on the side of a road in Argentina are gifts to an unofficial popular saint, la Difunta Correa, who died of thirst in the desert. MICHELLE MULDER

If given a choice, most people wouldn't drink this water, but even water that looks clean can be dangerous. Parasites and chemical pollution are often invisible and deadly. CAWST (CENTRE FOR AFFORDABLE WATER & SANITATION TECHNOLOGY)

What are your options if you don't have a water treatment plant nearby? These kids in El Salvador rely on a biosand filter, which cleans water the same way a natural wetland does. More about that in Chapter Three. CAWST

Wetlands can be overwhelmed though. In the eighteenth and nineteenth centuries, people created so much pollution with farming and other industries that the wetlands couldn't handle it. The swamps were swamped!

So people began looking for ways to clean the pollution out of their water before drinking it. In 1804, the town of Paisley in Scotland built the world's first citywide municipal water treatment plant. The plant used a sand filter system to clean the water before pumping it to people's homes. In other words, Paisley built a water-cleaning factory that worked just like a wetland. Now, many cities and towns around the world have systems for cleaning the water before it reaches people's homes.

But we keep dumping more waste into the water. Each day people dump 1.8 billion kilograms (2 million tons) of waste into waterways. Toxic chemicals from landfills, factories and mining, as well as garbage, sewage and acid rain, all pollute our water. Meanwhile, since the year 1900, we've drained, paved over, or otherwise destroyed half of the world's wetlands. Clean water is getting harder and harder to find.

CHECK OUT THESE PIPES!

The clean, fresh water that comes out of your tap may have had a long, complicated journey to your house. Chances are, it began in a reservoir—a big, human-made lake used to collect water. From there, the water likely drained through a mixture of sand and gravel to filter out dirt (in a water treatment plant—another one of those human-made wetlands). Next, chemicals like chlorine might have been poured in to kill any remaining germs. Only then does the water pour into big pipes that lead to your town or city. The pipes, called *mains*, run under streets and then through smaller pipes to buildings. Finally, even smaller pipes lead to your sink, toilet and bathtub.

Water that goes down drains or toilets flows out of the building to an underground sewer main. From there, it likely flows to a wastewater treatment plant. Screens filter out large solids, and depending on where you live, the poop is dumped into a sewage landfill or burned for energy. Gravity and finer filters remove smaller solids before the liquid pours into basins where bacteria eat up any remaining organic matter. (That's the polite way of saying "little bits of poop that escaped all those filters.") Sometimes chemicals or ultraviolet light might give the water its final "scrub" before it flows back out into the world's rivers, lakes and oceans. Wastewater plants help keep the world's water clean. Many places choose not to build them though, because they're so expensive.

Water treatment can be as simple as a sand filter, or as complex as this water treatment facility. NOSTAL6IE/DREAMSTIME.COM

WATER FACT: Water can carry disease, but with a bit of soap, it also gives us one of the easiest ways to prevent illness.

Go with the Flow

For a long time, when I traveled, I proudly wore a Canadian flag pin on my jacket. But in Esquel, Argentina, people glared at me, and I soon learned that a Canadian mining company was exploring the area to develop a gold mine. Across the city, citizens were holding meetings about the arsenic used in this exploration and discussing how that poison might filter into the drinking water. Horrified at the idea of being mistaken for a water-poisoner, I took off my Canadian pin, and people started smiling at me in the streets again.

Around the world, people are resisting Canadian mining companies whose mining techniques could poison local drinking water. This graffiti says "No to the mine." MICHELLE MULDER

Ever wondered what goes on underground? The Paris Sewer Museum (Le Musée des Égouts de Paris) offers visitors a chance to explore a sewer system that dates right back to 1370. (Nose plugs not included.) RAPHAËL GALICHER

And at this point, maybe you're wondering why we poop into water in the first place. Wouldn't it be easier to keep the world's water clean if we didn't? More about alternatives in Chapter Four.

THE WATER DRAIN

Around the world, people are talking about a water crisis. As both human population and industry grow, we need more and more fresh water. But climate change means water supplies are harder to predict. Technology that allows us to pump water out of aquifers means that many of them are emptying completely. (They'll take thousands of years to fill up again.) And harmful chemicals from mining and other industries, as well as sewage, are polluting more and more of our drinking water supply. Less and less of Earth's water is clean and available to drink.

That's why people around the world have thought up clever ways to get—and clean—that all-important liquid. And kids play a big role in that process. In many cultures, kids are the ones who gather the water for their families. In other places, like North America, kids often teach adults how to protect our water for future generations.

Engineers hope to tow large icebergs to the dry country of Saudi Arabia as a new source of fresh drinking water. (Meanwhile, other countries already tow fresh water across the sea in a different form. Ships from the Greek mainland drag enormous bags of fresh water to the Greek islands.) MICHELLE MULDER

WATER FACT: Forty-three percent of the world's population—that's almost three billion people—do not have water taps in their houses or even nearby.

Ganges River, in India and Bangladesh, is one of the world's most polluted rivers. Yet millions of people depend on its water for their daily needs. These Hindu pilgrims are bathing in the river as part of a religious festival. NEELSKY/SHUTTERSTOCK.COM

CHAPTER THREE

Pump It Up

DROP BY DROP

Kids in Zambia bring home water for their families. CAWST

Did you know that when you graduate from high school, it'll be partly thanks to your kitchen tap? In many countries, women and children walk up to six hours every single day, looking for a lake, stream, river, water hole, tap or well. They bring water home in any kind of container they can carry. Walking all those hours every day to get water doesn't leave kids much time or energy for school.

Let's say you're one of those kids and you're determined to get an education. Your parents treat the water with chlorine, but that doesn't kill all the germs (or *microbes*, as scientists call them) in the water, and the germs make you sick. If you recover—which you might not—you're likely to get sick from the water again before you grow up. You'll miss a lot of school, and as you've probably heard adults say a bazillion times, if you don't go to school, you can't get a good job later. Without a good job, you'll never be able to afford a home with a tap and clean water. Your story will likely repeat itself with your own children... unless something happens to change all that.

Sometimes even finding drinking water is dangerous. Imagine braving this water hole in Kenya each day!
THE RYAN'S WELL FOUNDATION/WWW.RYANSWELL.CA

This isn't just a random puddle. It's a source of drinking water for a small community in Cambodia. CAWST

Jimmy and Ryan, whose friendship changed the world! THE RYAN'S WELL FOUNDATION/ WWW.RYANSWELL.CA

WATER FACT: One in six people don't have access to clean water. Almost half of those people live in Africa.

MAKING CHANGE

In 1998, when Ryan Hreljac was in first grade in Canada, he learned about kids in Africa who grew up without clean water. Shocked, he decided to save money to build a well for a village in that faraway place. For months, he saved, talked to people about what he wanted to do and accepted donations. By 1999, he had raised enough money to build his well, and when he was nine, he visited Angolo Primary School in Uganda and saw how his well had changed lives. In 2001, Ryan and his family started the Ryan's Well Foundation, and now they've built over 740 wells and over 990 latrines, bringing safe water and improved health to more than 789,000 people in 16 countries.

Around the world, kids and adults are working hard to provide clean water, and clean water is saving lives.

GETTING THE NASTIES OUT

So you've got your water from the nearest well or water tap. Now how do you clean it? Boiling would get rid of the microbes, but what if your family can't afford—or can't find—fuel to heat the water? In Haiti, for example, deforestation has made wood scarce. People have barely enough to cook with, never mind extra for boiling drinking water.

If you can't boil your water, you're going to need a filter. One popular variety works like a mini-wetland in a corner of your kitchen. Once a day, a family member pours water into a concrete or plastic container. Inside, layers of gravel and sand trap any solid bits and dangerous microbes. Then helpful bacteria and other micro-organisms in the top two centimeters (less than an inch) of the sand chow down on the microbes. Within an hour, a biosand filter cleans twelve to eighteen liters (between three and five gallons) of water. Biosand filters remove over 90 percent of microbes, and the filters can last over twenty years.

But what if your family is nomadic? No one wants to haul around a concrete box full of gravel and sand every time they head for the hills. A clay pot is easy to carry along though. Potters make ceramic filters by mixing terra-cotta clay with sawdust or rice husks. Then they stretch the clay to form a pot. Baking burns away the sawdust or rice husks in the clay, leaving behind pores so tiny that they trap microbes and other particles. A bacteria-killing silver coating on the pot removes even more, leaving water 98 to 100 percent microbe-free.

Simple technology like these filters can get rid of most little creatures that cause diarrhea. And since diarrhea is one of the biggest killers in poor countries, filters are a real lifesaver!

NAILING THE PROBLEM

Ceramic filters are great for getting rid of bacteria, but what about other pollutants in the water? In Bangladesh and parts of India, for example, many people's drinking water has arsenic in it. Arsenic is a tasteless, odorless, colorless poison that occurs naturally in the ground in some places. In Bangladesh, up to 20 percent of all adult deaths are because of arsenic poisoning in the water.

A regular biosand filter doesn't help against arsenic, but add a pile of iron nails, and the arsenic sticks to the iron, leaving water safe to drink. Regularly replacing the nails keeps the filter working well. But the Centre for Affordable Water Sanitation Technology (CAWST) recommends that people bury the old nails away from any water source. No one wants the nails that cleaned their family's water to poison anyone else's!

VARONES

A simple latrine like this can stop diseases like cholera, which spreads through water contaminated by human feces. (Yup, folks, that's poo.) Cholera kills 130,000 people every year. A clean bathroom when you need one really is a lifesaver. MICHELLE MULDER

A sip of clean water thanks to a biosand filter in Afghanistan. CAWST

In Gaviotas, Colombia, the seesaw at the preschool is actually a water pump, and kids at the playground help pump water for their school and families by playing.
CENTRO LAS GAVIOTAS

Ceramic filters are easy to make and cheap to buy. They can purify up to three liters (less than a gallon) of water every hour.
POTTERS WITHOUT BORDERS

DRINKING THE OCEAN

So, if you lived in Uganda, your water glass might have deadly microbes in it. If you lived in Bangladesh, you might be drinking arsenic. And if you lived in the Gaza Strip, you might be filling your water glass with water from the ocean!

In some places, especially in the Middle East, factories called *desalination plants* force the salt out of the seawater, either by heating the salt water until it evaporates into another container, leaving the salt behind, or by forcing the salt water through a membrane with tiny holes that separate out the salt. But the technology and the fuel for these factories are expensive. Only the richest countries can afford them. Another drawback is the impact of desalination plants on the environment. Burning fossil fuels to make seawater drinkable contributes to global warming. And the salt left behind is often tossed back into the ocean. Close to shore, the water can become too salty, killing many local sea creatures.

The non-profit organization Green Empowerment uses sustainable energy to provide clean water to communities around the world, like this one in Nicaragua.
GREEN EMPOWERMENT/EVAN SABOGAL

On a small scale, though, desalination can keep people alive without killing anything else. In the Kalahari Desert, in Botswana, people often dig wells only to find salt water underground. But in the past thirty years, more and more families have been using small desalinating devices that run on sunshine. The sun evaporates water into a closed container. The water condenses at the top and slides down a slope into another container, ready to drink. Families use the remaining salt for cooking, preserving meat and curing animal skins. Fresh water, with no harm done to the environment!

The oceans aren't Earth's only salty spots. Many places have salt water underground, and on this salt plain in Salta, Argentina, the ground is entirely covered in salt. People chop it out in blocks and sell it for cooking. GASTÓN CASTAÑO

SIPPING SEWAGE

Imagine you're running an entire country. Fresh water is scarce, and there's no way you can afford desalination plants. How are you going to keep your people from dying of thirst?

WATER FACT: Desalination provides about 98 percent of Dubai's fresh water. The country has minimal rainfall, no rivers and little usable ground water.

Go with the Flow

Most people in Bolivia don't have hot water tanks to warm water for their showers. Instead, many install electric devices that heat the water as it comes through the showerhead. Usually, these devices deliver not only warm water but also a huge electric jolt to the person showering. In the hostels where we stayed, the shared bathroom was quite a distance from our room, but I could always tell when it was my husband's turn to shower because I recognized his shouts—either from the electric jolt when he braved the heating contraption, or from the ice-cold water when the contraption didn't work!

Electric showers can be just as shocking as they sound! Check out the scorch marks on the wall.
PETER HART

How strong is your stomach? In 2010, the Exploratorium science museum in San Francisco featured this drinking fountain as part of an exhibit. The fun part was watching people's faces when they thought about drinking from a toilet. ALEX DUNNE

WATER FACT: If your toilet was built before 1996, you likely use 13 to 20 liters (4 to 5 gallons) of water every time you flush. Low-flush toilets use only 6 liters (less than 2 gallons) per flush. Either way, the average North American household uses most of its drinking water to get rid of waste.

Brothers share a laugh at a water tap in Rwanda. SOLAR ELECTRIC LIGHT FUND (SELF)

In Namibia, water is so scarce that the government has built water treatment plants that make drinking water out of, yup, sewage. The country is one of the driest on the planet, and its population is growing like never before. The people of Windhoek, Namibia, have been drinking their own recycled wastewater since 1968. A lot of people are disgusted by the idea and buy bottled water instead of drinking from the tap, but ironically, the city is one of the few in Africa where the tap water is safe to drink.

And the Namibians aren't the only ones drinking recycled water. Singapore and parts of the United States are also starting to flush their toilets toward their taps. Many people around the world believe that treating and recycling our water is the way of the future.

ALL BOTTLED UP

A lot of people would rather drink bottled water than tap water—even if their water *doesn't* come from a sewage treatment plant! Yet at least a quarter of all bottled water is just tap water with a fancy label. It costs more than tap water does, but it isn't necessarily cleaner or safer. Worse, factories use plenty of petroleum (oil) to make the plastic bottles, and most of them get tossed into the landfill after only one use.

Bottled water raises another enormous question too. Is it right for bottled water companies to "own" water and sell it to others? A few years ago, the city of Cochabamba, Bolivia, chose to let a private company run all of its water systems. Suddenly, water prices skyrocketed. Riots broke out. People began collecting rainwater from their own roofs to drink. And the company demanded they buy permits to do that, since the company was in charge of *all* the city's water, even the rain! The local government ended the contract with that company, and the rain belongs to the people again.

Other water companies in other places have announced that they own certain glaciers, rivers and lakes, and those announcements aren't very well received. The water companies defend themselves by saying that water is a resource just like wood or oil, which are commonly bought and sold. But is it really the same? No one will die without wood or oil, but water is an absolute necessity for life. Should anyone really be allowed to decide who can to have it, based on how much they can pay?

SPOT ON

Stretching back in time, local water supplies have always been managed by local people. Our ancestors knew how to manage rivers and other water supplies very well. Small groups, not emperors or big businesses, managed water in each place. If we remember and re-teach what our ancestors knew, and if small groups focus on the kinds of water available in each spot on Earth, the future could be as refreshing as…well…a glass of cold water.

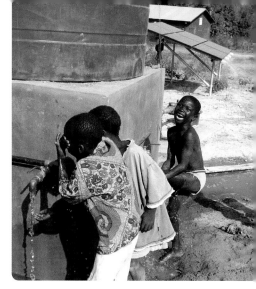

The Solar Electric Light Fund (SELF) brings solar panels to places that could never afford them and uses solar power to run everything from water pumps to medical clinics. These boys are enjoying one of SELF's projects in Benin.
SOLAR ELECTRIC LIGHT FUND (SELF)

Go with the Flow

When I visited my uncle in Germany when I was nine, I was perplexed by how each toilet seemed different from the last. I often had trouble finding the button, lever or pull-chain to flush. Later, I came across even more surprising toilets. In Bolivia, we flushed by pouring in jugs of water from a rain barrel. In Turkey, we squatted over a porcelain hole in the ground and sprayed it down with a hose afterward, and on trains across Argentina, pressing the lever on the toilet emptied the contents onto the tracks below!

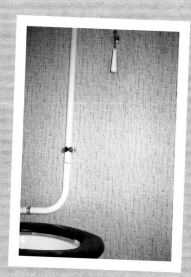

When I was nine, it took me a while to figure out how to flush my uncle's toilet. Who knew I had to pull a chain?
MICHELLE MULDER

Deepening the Well

FLUSHED WITH PRIDE

When Mexico City began running out of drinking water in the 1980s, city officials brainstormed solutions and found answers in the toilet. Every day most of us with flush toilets use a quarter of our drinking water to wash away waste. Mexico City launched a program to replace conventional toilets with toilets that use two-thirds less water for every flush. By 1991, Mexico City was saving 7.4 billion liters (about two billion gallons) of drinking water every year.

Meanwhile, some people wonder if we even need to flush at all. Why are we using drinking water to poop into? Probably because flush toilets stink less than latrines, where human waste decomposes in a hole in the ground. Latrines aren't the only water-free toilet option, though. *Compost toilets* have two containers, one that you sit on and the other that does the composting. Once you've done your business, you toss in lime (a form of calcium), ash, sawdust or wood chips. This smothers the stink, and eventually you'll be able to add your toilet's compost to the garden to grow next summer's salads, tomatoes and corn on the cob. From yuck to yum, without a drop of wasted water!

For a stink-free compost toilet, all you need is a hole in the ground, a bucket of leaves, soil or sawdust, and you're ready for...um...business. Simple, effective and water-free. MICHELLE MULDER

READY, SET...RAIN!

In some parts of the world, rain falls so hard that more than half the water runs along the surface of the soil without ever soaking in. Anagha Ann Gopakumar grew up in Aluva, India, where most of the rain falls in just 100 hours each year. She'd watched the annual monsoons all her life, and the cycle was always the same: monsoon, flood, drought. She felt sorry for the local farmers.

When she was ten, she began reading books and websites about water. Then her grandmother told her that farmers used to collect rainwater to use later in the year. So Anagha clambered up to her roof to set up a rainwater harvesting system. She used bamboo gutters that funneled rain into a container.

In many parts of the world, farmers face floods from monsoons and then months of drought. This farm is in India.
PIXELAPPEAL/DREAMSTIME.COM

Boys off to find water for their families in Laos. JIM HOLMES

Stop! Catch that rain! Rain barrels can save families hundreds of liters of water every year. ZYGIMANTAS CEPAITIS/ SHUTTERSTOCK.COM

Pebbles and charcoal helped filter the water into a pipe that ran to a well. The next time the monsoons came, she collected enough water for her family and for some of the local farmers too. Then she taught them how to build their own systems. In 2006, she won an International Young Eco-Hero Award for environmental achievement.

GULPING WEATHER

Did you know that farmers can shape their fields to catch more rain?

In the 1970s, in Laporiya Village on the edge of Thar Desert in India, people and their cattle were getting thirsty. It didn't seem to be raining any less than before, but more of the rain was running off the land and away from fields and wells. Worried, almost half the families moved away to places with more water, but the families who stayed decided to restore the water harvesting system that their ancestors had used, a system that people had forgotten about over the years.

These days, dikes surround each pasture, and those pastures are sloped, so if one receives more rain than it needs, water flows down to the next. Eventually, excess water collects in a deep village pond, where people can come get it. In the past few decades, local well water has become fifteen meters (sixteen yards) deeper, and crops are producing three to twelve times more food, all because people remembered the simple farming techniques of a few generations ago.

Imagine if all the water used by golf greens went to people instead. SEESEA/DREAMSTIME.COM

WATER FACT: Earth is home to a lot of golf courses. And those green lawns need plenty of water. In fact, the world's golf courses consume 9.5 billion liters (2.5 billion gallons) of water every day. That's enough clean water to quench the thirst of 500 million people.

These women in Kenya are planting trees to stop soil erosion and water runoff. By planting trees, the people of Kenya have turned much of their country from dry, barren dust into rich agricultural land. THE GREEN BELT MOVEMENT

THIRSTY? PLANT A TREE

Runoff doesn't only happen on hot, arid farmland. It also happens in cities, where rain can't soak into the soil because the ground is covered in pavement. Forests cover about 30 percent of Earth's land, but we're cutting down our trees fast, mostly so we can build buildings or roads. The more we chop, the more rain rolls along Earth's surface instead of soaking into it.

Why is that a big deal? Rain does more than just water plants. It also soaks into the ground to refill aquifers, those natural underground pools that so many rely on for water. We're draining them quickly, and they take thousands of years to refill.

What to do? Plant a tree! Or several! Trees and their roots act like little dikes, trapping the water in one place so that it can soak into the ground. Sure, the trees will use some of the rainwater, but in general, the more trees and plants we've got, the more water will soak into the soil instead of escaping sideways. Imagine what the world would be like if every single person planted a tree, or two or three.

In the 1970s, Professor Wangari Maathai watched people struggle to find firewood, grow food and find water in Kenya. She encouraged women to plant trees and, by doing so, changed the entire future of her country. Where trees grow, water can sink into the ground, and where there's water, there's life.
THE GREEN BELT MOVEMENT

A girl stands in front of a water tank and two large FogQuest fog collectors on a farm in Tojquia, Guatemala. FOGQUEST/MELISSA ROSATO

FOG IN YOUR CUP

What if you've already tried every water-harvesting technique you know and planted trees galore, but you're still thirsty? Try harvesting fog! In Africa and South America, people have been doing it for thousands of years: fog condenses onto leaves, and people either shake it into containers or drink it on the spot.

A Canadian nonprofit organization decided to use modern technology to harvest fog for the mountain village of Chungungo, Chile. Until 1992, villagers struggled to collect enough drinking water to survive. Then FogQuest set up ninety-four big nets made of inexpensive, durable plastic mesh on nearby El Tofo Mountain. Each net stretches between two wooden poles above a trough on the ground that's connected to pipes leading to the village.

These days, an average of 15,000 liters (almost 4,000 gallons) of water a day pours down from the fog catchers. The local people have even started growing gardens and fruit trees with all the water they've got flowing down from their misty mountainside. FogQuest has projects around the world.

DROPS BY THE BUCKETFUL

In Matamoros, Mexico, the local government solved its water problems by using a different natural resource: kid power! Sometimes it might not seem like kids have much say in how the world works, but kids teach the adults in their lives a lot. That's why the government of Matamoros created a program called the Water Detectives. First, they taught kids how to conserve water. Then they gave them badges announcing their important roles. Teams of water detectives visited houses and businesses throughout the city. They talked to adults about

Kids in Matamoros, Mexico, take water conservation seriously. And thanks to them, adults do too.
COURTESY OF NATIONAL FILM BOARD/DAVID SPRINGBELT

How do you wash your hands in a place without running water? Tippy taps like this one are becoming more and more popular around the world. Step on a lever or a string, and a tiny bit of water comes out—just enough to rinse soapy hands, and no more. Simple technology can save water and save lives at the same time. CAWST

repairing leaky pipes and using dishwashing or laundry water for gardening and car washing. The result? One year later, the city's citizens were using 18 percent less water. That's almost a fifth of the water supply saved, thanks to kids!

You can make a big difference to the world's water supply even without an official badge. And you can begin right where you live. Here are some ideas to get you started.

Save water

Turn off dripping faucets. Fix leaks. Take a five-minute shower instead of a bath. Use a watering can instead of a hose for your garden. Experiment with water harvesting and set up a rain barrel. Put a water-saving device in your toilet tank and save 750 liters (almost 200 gallons) of water a year!

Keep it clean

A lot of the products we use wind up in the water. Whenever possible, help your family choose nontoxic chemicals for

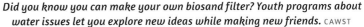

Did you know you can make your own biosand filter? Youth programs about water issues let you explore new ideas while making new friends. CAWST

cleaning at home. Avoid pesticides, and find out where you can dispose of toxic liquids responsibly, instead of pouring them down the drain.

Kids at the CAWST Youth Wavemakers Summit in Calgary, Canada, learn about water, sanitation and hygiene, and how to take action. CAWST

Give the water cycle a helping hand

Choose tap water over bottled water. Plant trees. Cultivate an edible garden instead of grass (which needs a lot of water and doesn't taste nearly as good!). If you're not into vegetables, planting native plants instead of grass can save water. Native plants get all the water they need from the rain.

Spread the word

Tell your friends what you know about water. Write to people in power who can have a major impact on the world's water. The mining companies of Canada and the United States, for example, are responsible for a big chunk of water pollution around the world. (Canada is home to 70 percent of the world's mining companies!) Ask them to use responsible mining techniques to keep poisons out of our waterways.

Eating fruits or vegetables washed in dirty water makes many people sick. This girl is washing lettuce in Laos. JIM HOLMES

Pass it on

Raise money for wells, latrines or water filters in other parts of the world. (Check out the "Resources" section of this book for some websites that might help.) Join thousands of kids worldwide who are just as passionate about water as you are.

THE RIPPLE EFFECT

Way back in Chapter One, we saw how the Minoans had running water and flush toilets 3,600 years ago, and then for the next several centuries, people in the very same region forgot about plumbing. Later, the Romans built a big sewer system under Rome, and a few centuries afterward, people forgot how to do that too. Times change. Each society values different things.

WATER FACT: In many places in North America, families use 30 percent more water in the summertime to water gardens and lawns. Using water from rain barrels would save each household over 3,785 liters (1,000 gallons) of water in those hot summer months.

Once Mr. Watt developed his steam engine in the 1700s, humans had easy access to more water than ever before. It no longer seemed like such a precious resource. But the world's clean water supply is limited, and it's time to change the way we think about water.

Since the first humans walked the earth, people have risen to the challenge of finding, cleaning and conserving water. These days, we've got both the knowledge of the past and the technology of the present to help us with this challenge. With creative thinking and a whole lot of teamwork, who knows what exciting developments the future will bring?

No matter where you live, every drop of water is precious. These children in Vietnam are moving water to a school tank for a new latrine block. JIM HOLMES

Go with the Flow

Camping at Parque de los Glaciares in Argentina was a treat. Not only was it gorgeous, but we didn't have to bring a drop of water with us! A big glacier feeds the park's lakes and streams, providing some of the freshest, cleanest water you'll ever drink. Anyone found washing, peeing or pooing within ten meters (about ten yards) of a lake or stream is fined and kicked out of the park. Imagine if everyone treated the planet's water with such respect!

When hiking in Parque de los Glaciares, Argentina, we filled our water bottles in the nearest stream.
MICHELLE MULDER

Soon this girl's community in El Balsamo, Nicaragua, will have water piped directly to its homes, allowing kids like Dania more time to go to school.
GREEN EMPOWERMENT/ SHERRI PHILLIPS

Resources

Books

Spilsbury, Louise. *Running Water: Our Most Precious Resource.*
Chicago, IL: Raintree, 2006.
Woodward, John. *Water.* New York, NY: DK Publishing, 2009.

Movies

Springbett, David. *Water Detectives.* Montreal, QC:
National Film Board of Canada, 2007.

Websites

FogQuest: http://www.fogquest.org
Green Belt Movement: http://www.greenbeltmovement.org
Green Empowerment: http://www.greenempowerment.org
H₂OUSE Water Saver Home: http://www.h2ouse.net
Potters Without Borders:
http://www.potterswithoutborders.com
Ryan's Well Foundation: http://www.ryanswell.ca
Solar Electric Light Fund (SELF): http://www.self.org
Wavemakers—CAWST's Youth Program:
http://www.wavemakers.cawst.org

Acknowledgments

One of the greatest pleasures of writing this book has been to receive emails from people around the world offering information, contact details and photos. I have a long list of people to thank, beginning with Melanie Fricot, whose salty banana milkshakes and ride to the hospital saved my life, and whose friendship is one of the reasons I love my life so much! Thanks, too, to David Johnson, Rosa Villón and the people of Pamparomas, Peru, who gave me a whole new appreciation of water and solidarity.

I'm grateful for Brian Fagan's book *Elixir: A History of Water and Humankind*, which gave me glimpses into cultures I knew nothing about. Thank you to Shauna Curry, Michelle MacDonald, Emilie Sanmartin and Natasha Sarkar of CAWST (Centre for Affordable Water and Sanitation Technology), whose support, enthusiasm and assistance with photos and information were invaluable in getting this book written.

Thanks to Solar Electric Light Fund, Ryan's Well Foundation and Potters Without Borders for sharing a wealth of photos. For spectacular images, contacts and information from around the world, I send thanks to Melanie Fricot, Gastón Castaño, Henry Mulder, Susie Mullen, Sherri Phillips, Evan Sabogal, Dr. Abul Hussam, Dr. Abul Munir, Bob McInnes, Paolo Lugari, Terry Spragg, Kai Morrill, Elisabeth Rubli, Jane Baird, Robert Schemenauer, Katie Hammel, John Alejandro, Jim Holmes, David Springbett, Heather MacAndrew, Peter Hart, Ian Paul and Alex Dunne. (Thanks, too, to all the kids who agreed to have their photos published in a children's book!)

I am grateful to Orca Book Publishers for the opportunity to write this. Many thanks to Sarah Harvey for her guidance and insightful editing, and to Jenn Playford and Teresa Bubela for their beautiful book design.

Thanks to Maia-who-knows-how-to-swim for her patience as I wrote this book, to Liam and Sam for keeping her company, and to Ashley for her help with childcare in the final days of rewrites.

I especially want to thank all the members of my family who cheered me on, even when I brought up disgusting facts about Roman communal toilet sponges (*blech!*) over dinner. You really are a patient lot.

Thank you, everyone.

These boys are doing one of the most important jobs in their family—bringing clean water home. HEL080808/DREAMSTIME.COM

Index

*Page numbers in **bold** indicate an image; there may also be text related to the same topic on that page*

J 333.91 M

Every last drop

Mulder, Michelle.
$19.95   **3201300192474**

2/15 2x			

5/14